The Flowers of Central

Alec M. Blombery

 J.B. BOOKS AUSTRALIA

This edition published in Australia in 2001 by:
J.B. Books Pty. Ltd.
P.O. Box 118
Marleston 5033
South Australia
Phone: (08) 8351 1688
Fax: (08) 8351 1699

First published in 1989 by Kangaroo Press Pty Ltd
Reprinted 1992
Revised edition printed 2001

© Alec M. Blombery

All rights reserved. No part of this publication may be reproduced, stored in a retrieval system, or transmitted, in any form or by any means, electronic, mechanical, photocopying, recording or otherwise, without the prior permission of the publisher in writing.

ISBN 1 876 622 318

Revision: Alec Blombery
Editing: Ann Peisley and John Brakel

Produced by Phoenix Offset. Printed in Hong Kong

Introduction

The flora of Central Australia has evolved to its present state over millions of years by adapting to the extreme conditions to which it has been subjected. As a result of these conditions the plants have developed various characteristics which make them ideally suited to their environment.

To assist in understanding the plants of Central Australia a consideration of the various factors which influence the growth of plants will be found helpful.

Climate

The availability of water and temperature are the chief factors governing plant growth, together with the nature of the soil and topography.

Rainfall

For the purpose of this discussion Alice Springs is taken as the approximate centre of Australia.

The average rainfall of the Alice Springs and surrounding area is regarded as approximately 10 inches or 250 mm. Although the rainfall is taken as an average this is measured over a long period. At one extreme there may be periods of up to 10 years when the area receives no rain. Conversely there may be periods when the area is subjected to torrential rains, when dry watercourses become raging torrents with flooding occurring over adjoining plain areas. Between the two extremes there may be periods when rain is received each year, frequently falling in February and March. Areas north of Alice Springs come more under the influence of the northern monsoonal rains, resulting in a higher average rainfall. South of Alice Springs the average rainfall becomes less, reducing to 5 inches or 125 mm around the Lake Eyre area. Throughout these areas there may be localities which, due to some topographical feature, receive more or less rainfall.

Sunlight

Being well removed from the sea, Central Australia usually experiences little cloud cover. Records show that 80% of possible is received. As a result of this large amount of sunshine the evaporation rate is extremely high and rapidly dries out moisture from all exposed areas and to a lesser extent from protected areas.

Physical Characters and Topography

Central Australia is a vast area of sandy and stony plains, low lying depressions, sand dunes, and undulating hills with numerous rocky outcrops. Plain areas may be interrupted by large isolated eminences such as Mt Connor and Ayers Rock. The extensive and picturesque MacDonnell Ranges, in which Alice Springs is situated, consist of a number of separate mountain ranges which are intersected by valleys and gorges. These, together with the rocky outcrops, provide shaded areas which can give some protection from the ever present sunlight. The rocks, being impervious, shed rainfall on to the surrounding ground, thus increasing the available moisture in the close adjoining area. Around Ayers Rock there is a much denser growth of trees and shrubs than is found on the plain area where only direct rainfall is received. In the rocky gullies there are frequently deep depressions which hold water; due to the protected nature of these positions, evaporation is much reduced and water remains for extended periods. These pools may also be fed by springs from underground water.

In the large watercourses there is a considerable depth of sand and rocky debris built up over a very long period, and beneath this debris there is usually water present at various depths in depressions in the river bed bottom. On plain areas there are depressions in the ground with an impervious base, which over long periods have been filled with drifting sands and other debris. These depressions hold water for periods of flooding rains and thus serve as reservoirs of underground water. Being protected from evaporation, these may remain for indefinite periods. These sources of underground water enable large trees like the River Gum to grow in river beds without having to rely on regular rainfall. The depth of soil varies considerably on flat plain areas: where the soil is deep there is much more stored moisture. These deep soils and underground depressions explain why there are groups of shrubs and small trees in some areas and not in others.

Plant Adaption to Arid Conditions

Plants adopt various measures to deal with arid conditions. Various characteristics help reduce loss of moisture, for example the surfaces of the plant may be covered with a close covering of fine hairs which prevents air circulating close to the plant surfaces. Other plants have developed a coating of a varnishlike substance which prevents evaporation of moisture. Some plants, such as parakeela, have fleshy leaves beneath this coating, which enable the plant to store water. Also, leaves may be reduced in size, as in the Desert Oak where they occur as tiny scales around narrow branchlets. Other leaves are hard and cylindrical with a hard point to resist drying, as in the Corkwood. Still others may be divided into narrow segments as in the cassia and many other plants. To reduce evaporation of moisture many plants, such as the eucalypts and mulga, present the edges of their leaves to the sun rather than the flat surface.

Types of Plants

Plants may be classified according to their habit of growth.

Ephemeral or Annual Plants

These plants have seed which can resist heat and drying for long periods and still remain viable. When rains come the seed germinates rapidly, sometimes within a few days. The resultant seedling grows quickly and may flower within a month or two while there is still moisture in the ground. Seed develops rapidly and when ripe falls; if sufficient moisture is present this seed will germinate in its turn, with the process being repeated until moisture no longer remains. Once there is insufficient moisture the seed remains in a dormant state on the ground for an indefinite period until the next rain is received. The daisy family is a classical case of this form of growth, producing large quantities of seed. When there are several good seasons, these together with other species of plants turn vast areas into floral gardens of white, yellow, pink, red, lilac and blue and purple as far as the eye can see.

Perennial or Long Lived Plants

This group of plants grow as small to large shrubs or trees. When their seeds germinate, the roots grow deeply into the ground in search of a permanent source of moisture; if this is not available the developing plant soon dies. Extensive watercourses enable such large trees as the River Gum to grow, as the underground source of water tides the plant over extended periods of drought. As the roots are firmly and deeply anchored in the river bed, they are able to resist strong river flows during the periods of flooding rains. On sand plain areas groups of Mulga develop on deep soils over underground water and are not affected by drought. On flood plains there are deep layers of silty soil which hold moisture and large trees such as Coolabah and Gidgee develop. In order that the continued production of seed does not result in too many seedlings, actively growing plants produce inhibiting substances. When plants die or the area is flooded these inhibiting substances are washed away.

During periods of extended drought the plants may shed their leaves to reduce transpiration and more or less live in a state of dormancy, producing new leaves when rain comes. When there are very long periods of drought and the plant exhausts the supply of underground water it may even die. In such cases new plants grow from dormant seed. Another measure is that adopted by perennial grasses and plants such as the Rock Fern which grows in rock crevices such as at Ayers Rock, and the cloverlike nardoo fern. These plants completely die down and may remain in a state of dormancy for an indefinite period. When rains come, within a few days the plants come to life and grow rapidly again.

Other plants such as the Cabbage Palm, *Livistona mariae*, and the cycad *Macrozamia macdonnellii* are very ancient or relic plants which were widespread when the climate of Central Australia had a more equable high rainfall. In order to exist these plants have retreated to favourable locations, for example the Cabbage Palm or Mariae Palm only grows in Palm Valley and other tributaries of the upper Finke River where there is permanent water. The cycad Macrozamia Palm occurs in deep gorges where it grows in shaded areas. Other plants also take advantage of these favourable protected locations, amongst them the Cypress Pine, the yellow flowered *Hibbertia glaberima*, the mint bush *Prostanthera striatiflora* and *Rulingia grandiflora* which is found only at the bottom of deep shaded gorges such as Kings Canyon.

The plants described are a good representation of plants commonly seen and more likely to be observed. Naturally costs make it impracticable to illustrate all the different plants which appear at different times in the area.

Hibiscus Family, Malvaceae

Hibiscus Found in warmer parts of the world including Australia. The commercial cotton plant belongs to this family.
Hibiscus sturtii An erect shrub 0.5 to 1 m high, leaves greyish green egg to lance shaped. Flowers large white to pink with a darker centre apex of projecting style divided into 5. Occurs on sandy gravelly or rocky slopes.

Gossypium This genus, which includes the Northern Territory emblem, resembles *Hibiscus* but the style is twisted and not divided.
Gossypium sturtianum Sturts Desert Rose An erect shrub 1 to 2 m high, leaves smooth spotted egg shaped, flowers pinkish lilac with a deep red centre.

Hibiscus sturtii

Sturts Desert Rose

Occurs along watercourses in rocky sandy gravelly soils.
Gossypium australe A shrub 1 to 2 m high, leaves greyish green elliptical, spotting less distinct, flowers white to pink with deep red centre. Occurs in sandy gravelly and rocky soils.

Gossypium australe

Radyera Closely resembles *Hibiscus*, but apex of projecting style enlarged and not divided.
Radyera farragei A small shrub to about 1 m, leaves smooth heart shaped, flowers purplish pink with a deeper centre. Occurs in areas subject to flooding, creek beds and roadsides.

Lavatera Found in warm parts of the world with one species in Australia.
Lavatera plebeia Native Hollyhock A slender plant 1 to 3 m high, leaves 5 to 7 lobed, flowers small, hibiscus-like, white to lilac in clusters. Occurs on areas subject to flooding in sandy soils and creek beds.

Sida These plants are closely allied to *Abutilon*, but the honeycomb-like seed case has only one seed to each seed chamber.
Sida petrophile An erect shrub, leaves greyish oblong to lance shaped with scalloped edges, flowers yellow in groups of one or two clusters at ends of branches. Occurs on rocky areas.

Abutilon Found in warmer parts of the world with a number cultivated. The central column of the flower is divided into a number of filaments, seed cases have several seeds in each seed chamber.

Abutilon leucopetalum A small spreading shrub, leaves soft greyish green round to egg shaped, edges scalloped, flowers small yellow single on slender stalks. Occurs on rocky slopes.

Abutilon fraseri An erect plant, leaves greyish green heart to egg shaped, flowers yellow single on slender stalks. Ocurs on rocky outcrops and rocky slopes.

Abutilon leucopetalum

The Daisies

Daisies are well represented in Central Australia. Although most of the daisies in the area die after flowering (ephemerals or annuals), the Spiked Daisy Bush and some of the Brachycome daisies live for indefinite periods (perennials) in favourable locations. Daisies produce large numbers of seed and after rains these germinate to literally carpet extensive areas in white, yellow, pinks and blues. When several seasons of good rains occur the coloured carpet intensifies.

Daisies differ from most flowers in that they consist of a large number of small tubular flowers crowded together, mostly without petals, surrounded at the base by a ring of modified leaves called bracts. To help understand the daisies, they can be simply divided into 3 groups. The typical daisies have a densely packed centre of petalless flowers with each of the outer ring of flowers having a soft strap-like coloured petal, as in the exotic gerbera. The paper daisies have a tightly packed centre of tubular flowers without petals, surrounded by numerous papery bracts—yellow, white, pink or brownish —resembling petals which close around the flowers when rain or moisture is present. The button daisies have the small tubular flowers packed into an almost globular head without any extending petals. However one genus has flowers which extend with rolled back lobes, the base being surrounded by small overlapping yellow bracts.

Crowsfoot *Erodium cygnorum* with small blue flowers and lobed leaves commonly occurs amongst massed daisies.

Typical Daisies

Senecio Flower heads with soft spreading yellow petals and white fluffy seeds.
Tall Yellow Top *Senecio magnificus* An erect fleshy plant to 1 m, leaves greyish broad fleshy stem clasping, flowers in clusters at end of stems. Occurs in sandy soil and often on edges of roads.
Yellow Top *Senecio gregorii* Similar to Tall Yellow Top but smaller. Leaves greyish narrow, flowers large single at top of stems. Occurs on sand plains and amongst mulga.
Variable Groundsel *Senecio lautus* A small plant 10 to 20 cm. Leaves narrow, dark green, flowerheads small in clusters. Occurs on a variety of soils.

Brachyscome Flowerheads small with centre of yellow flowers surrounded by a ring of soft white, pink or blue spreading petals and a shallow green hemispherical base of green bracts. Leaves entire or divided.
Swan River Daisy *Brachyscome iberidifolia* A small slender plant. Leaves narrow green. Flowerheads white, pink or blue. Occurs on sandy areas and along dry watercourses.
Variable Daisy *Brachyscome ciliaris* A small spreading bushy plant. Leaves divided. Flowerheads and white to purple petals. Occurs on sand and gibber plains and rocky areas.

Podolepis Flowerheads yellow, petals soft with divided ends, base hemispherical with overlapping close papery scales. Seeds with a fluffy top.
Showy Podolepis *Podolepis jaceoides* A small plant. Leaves linear to lance shaped chiefly at base. Flowerheads large yellow single at end of stem.

Calotis Flowerheads similar to Brachyscome, but seeds with sharp spines forming prickly burrs.
Blue Burr Daisy *Calotis cuneifolia* A small plant to about 20 cm. Leaves wedge shaped lobed. Flowerheads yellow

a Tall Yellow Top *Senecio magnificus*
b Variable Groundsel *Senecio lautus*
c Showy Podolepis *Podolepis jaceoides*
d Swan River Daisy *Brachyscome iberidifolia*
e Blue-burr Daisy *Calotis cuneifolia*

with blue petals. Occurs on sandy and clayey soils.

Bogan Flea *Calotis hispidula* A small spreading plant to 50 cm. Leaves narrow wedge shaped to lance shaped. Flowerheads with small yellow petals; seeds spiny and flea-like, with a similar irritating affect. Occurs on various soil types.

Minuria Flowerheads similar to Brachycome with yellow, white or pink petals; seeds with a few bristles.
Minnie Daisy *Minuria leptophylla* A compact cushion type plant. Leaves narrow. Flowerheads with numerous white to mauve petals. Occurs on sandy and rocky soils.

Olearia Shrubby plants; flowerheads with yellow centre, soft spreading petals, white to mauve; base cylindrical.
Spiked Daisy Bush *Olearia subspicata* An erect bushy shrub to 1.5 m high. Younger branches hoary; leaves linear, smooth above, woolly beneath. Flowerheads with white petals. Occurs on red sandy soil.
Pimelea Daisy Bush *Olearia pimeleoides* A small shrub usually less than 1 m. Younger branches white hoary. Leaves egg shaped to broad lance shaped, edges turned down, woolly beneath. Flowerheads single in clusters, petals white, flower base woolly. Occurs on rocky and sandy soils.

Fuzzweed, *Vittidinia* Small plants with small entire or lobed leaves. Flowerheads with short white to blue petals, flower base cylindrical seedheads fluffy. Occurs on various soils.

Paper Daisies

These daisies have a centre of small flowers surrounded by numerous bracts which close around the flowers when wet.

Bracteantha Flowerheads with stiff papery spreading petal like bracts; seedheads with white bristles with feathery apex.
Yellow Everlasting *Bracteantha bracteata* An erect to spreading plant 20 to 60 cm. Leaves soft, stem clasping, lance shaped. Flowerheads large with numerous stiff yellow shiny spreading papery bracts. Occurs on sand plains and rocky soils.
Schoenia cassinia with *Senecio gregorii* growing amongst mulga. Pink Everlasting *Helichrysum cassinianum* A slender plant 9 to 60 cm. Leaves greyish narrow, chiefly basal. Flowerheads with white to pinks spreading papery petal-like bracts. Occurs on sand plains often amongst mulga with Yellowtop, *Senecio gregorii*.
Yellow Everlasting *Helichrysum apiculatum* A slender plant with several stems arising from the ground. Leaves narrow greyish green. Flowerheads small with short yellow papery bracts in clusters. Occurs on rocky and sandy soils.

a Minnie Daisy *Minuria leptophylla*
b Spiked Daisy Bush *Olearia subspicata*
c Yellow Everlasting *Bracteantha bracteata*
d Helichyrsum, Senecio, Erodium
e Pink Everlasting *Schoenia cassinia*
f *Chrysocephalum apiculatum*

Rhodanthe This genus resembles *Helichrysum* but the papery bracts are usually softer, the seed is more angular and the 5 bristles at the top of the seed are feathery from the base to the apex.
Helipterum moschatum An erect woolly plant with a number of stems arising from the ground. Leaves narrow, stem clasping. Flowerheads very small surrounded by small yellow to straw coloured bracts in dense terminal clusters. Occurs on sandy soils.
White Paper Daisy *Rhodanthe floribunda* A small spreading plant 4 to 30 cm. Leaves narrow, chiefly at the base. Flowerheads with a yellow centre and numerous white papery petal-like bracts. Occurs chiefly on sand plains and amongst Mulga.
Yellow Everlasting *Leucochrysum stiputatum* A small erect to spreading plant. Leaves narrow woolly 40 to 60 cm. Flowerheads 30 mm across with numerous shiny paper yellow bracts. Occurs on sandy soil often amongst spinifex.
Cephalipterum drummondii A slender plant to 30 cm. Leaves narrow. Flowerheads consist of a number of small flowers with papery bracts of yellow, pink or white grouped together into a globular head. Occurs in sandy soil.

Myriocephalus This genus differs from the other paper daisies in that the yellow centre consists of small heads surrounded by close fitting papery bracts grouped together and surrounded by numerous small spreading petal-like papery bracts.
Poached egg Daisy *Myriocephalus stuartii* An erect woolly plant 10 to 20 cm. Leaves lance shaped. Flowerheads large with yellow centre and spreading white papery bracts. Occurs on sand plains and dunes.

Button Daisies

This group of daisies do not have spreading petals or bracts.

Pycnosorus This group has numerous heads of 3 to 10 tiny flowers enclosed in thin bracts, with a number forming a dense globular, oblong to egg shaped yellow head.
Billy Button *Pycnosorus chrysanthes* An erect woolly plant to 25 cm. Leaves narrow. Flowerheads yellow, oblong, 1 to 2.5 cm long, 1 cm diameter. Occurs on various types of soils.

Calocephalus Similar to *Pycnosorus* but there are no bracts between the groups of flowers and heads are globular.
Billy Button *Calocephalus platycephalus* A woolly plant to 45 cm. Leaves narrow woolly. Flowerheads yellow, globular 1 to 2 cm across. Occurs on sandy soil.

Pterocaulon This genus has a number of small flowers in a dense globular head with the ends of the flowers projecting.
Apple Bush *Pterocaulon sphacelatum* An erect rough plant. Leaves narrow rough, fruity aroma when crushed. Flowerheads pink globular to egg shaped. Occurs on sandy and clayey soils on flood and gibber plains.

Rutidosis This daisy has a number of single yellow flowers projecting with the lobes rolled back; the base is covered with numerous small overlapping bracts.
Grey Wrinklewort *Rutidosis helichrysoides* A variable woolly plant to 60 cm. Leaves long narrow woolly. Flowerheads bright yellow in clusters at top of branches. Occurs on sandy heavy soils.

a *Leucochrysum stipitatum*
b White Paper Daisy *Rhodanthe floribunda*
c *Cephalipterum drummondii*
d Poached-egg Daisy *Myriocephalus stuartii*

a Billy Buttons *Pyenosorus chrysanthes*
b *Calocephalus platycephalus*
c Apple Bush *Pterocaulon sphacelatum*
d Grey Wrinklwort *Rutidosis helichrysoides*

The Portulaca Family

The family is better known by the exotic cultivated portulaca. These plants have fleshy succulent leaves.

Portulaca pilosa A small spreading plant with broad fleshy leaves. Flowers in clusters, yellow with 5 spreading petals. Occurs on sandy and heavy soils.

Parakeela, *Calandrinia* A small group of plants with fleshy succulent foliage and flowers with 4 to 11 petals.

Round Leaved Parakeela *Calandrinia remota* A spreading plant with fleshy cylindrical leaves. Flowers shiny reddish purple (rarely white) in groups on long stems. Occurs on sandy loam, sand plains and dunes.

Broad Leaved Parakeela *Calandrinia balonensis* A low spreading plant. Leaves broad lance shaped fleshy. Flowers shiny reddish purple in groups at ends of long slender stems. Occurs on sandy loam, sand plains and dunes.

Pussy tails, mulla mullas, *ptilotus* These plants have a number of small fluffy flowers grouped into somewhat globular, cylindrical, conical, bottlebrush-like heads in creams and pinks.

Pink Mulla Mulla *Ptilotus exaltatus* An erect clump forming plant to about 1 m tall. Leaves lance to egg shaped smooth, fleshy. Flowerheads large deep pink cylindrical to conical. Occurs on rocky soils, sand ridges and amongst mulga.

Hairy Mulla Mulla *Ptilotus helipteroides* A small spreading plant. Leaves lance shaped silky hairy. Flowerheads pink globular to cylindrical. Occurs on hillsides and flat sandy or gravelly areas.

Large Green Pussytail *Ptilotus macrocephalus* A tufted plant with stems 30 cm to 1 m. Leaves narrow to lance shaped. Flowerheads cream to pale green, cylindrical to hemispherical. Occurs on various soils from red sandy to clayey and on rocky hillsides.

a

Round-leaved Parakeela *Calandrinia remota*
Broad-leaved Parakeela *Calandrinia balonensis*

b

a Pink Mulla Mulla *Ptilotus exaltatus*
b Hairy Mulla Mulla *Ptilotus helipteroides*
c Large Green Pussytail *Ptilotus macrocephalus*
d *Ptilotus macrocephalus*
e Long Tails *Ptilotus polystachys*

f   Silver Bush *Ptilotus obovatus*
g   *Achryanthes aspera*

Longtails, Bottlewashers *Ptilotus polystachus* A spreading clump forming plant. Leaves narrow to lance shaped. Flowerheads long cylindrical, often bent, yellowish green to red. Occurs on alluvial flats, gravelly and stony areas and along roadsides.

Silvertails *Ptilotus obovatus* A spreading variable plant 10 cm to 1m. Leaves woolly silvery grey egg to lance shaped. Occurs on a variety of soils.

Achyranthes This group of plants is found in warmer parts of the world; the one Australian species extends beyond Australia.

Achranthes aspera An erect plant with a number of stems arising from the ground. Leaves egg shaped light green soft. Flowers pink small, in long slender spikes. Occurs chiefly in rocky gullies.

Early Nancy, *Wurmbea* Small plants with fleshy leaves and small 6 petalled flowers.

Wurmbea centralis A small plant to 20 cm. Leaves narrow, lance shaped, soft fleshy, arising from the ground. Flowers pink, tubular at base, lobes spreading, in slender spikes. Occurs in sandy soil only in the Olgas.

Early Nancy *Wurmbea dioica* A small plant with several soft leaves. Flowers white to pink in short sprays. Occurs on moist sandy soils often in groups.

Grass Tree *Xanthorrhoea thorntonii* A plant with a stout trunk about 20 cm

a   Early Nancy *Anguillaria centralis*
b   Grass Tree *Xanthorrhoea thorntonii*

a Wild Stock *Blennodia canescens*
b *Blennodia canescens*

diameter, to 3 m high. Leaves stiff long angular and numerous, crowded in a dense head. Flowers tiny white 6 petalled, crowded into a dense stout long spike followed by sharp black seed capsules. Occurs in limited areas, on sand plains, e.g. Gosses Bluff area.

Blennodia Belonging to the cabbage family, these small plants have 4 petalled flowers followed by cylindrical seed pods with numerous seed.
Wild Stock *Blennodia canescens* A small erect plant with small lobed leaves. Flowers cream to pink, numerous in sprays. Occurs on sand plains, stony soils and dunes.

The Potato Family

This group of plants includes the potato, *Solanum tuberosum* and the tomato, *Lycopersicon lycopersicum*.

Solanum This genus is widespread throughout the world and includes poisonous species such as the Black Nightshade. Many of the species are very similar and require close examination to separate. The fruit of some species are eaten by Aborigines.
Wild Tomato *Solanum quadriloculatum* A spreading greyish plant with prickles on stems and leaves; leaves elliptical felty. Flowers purple in clusters. Fruit globular yellowish green. Occurs on sandy and rocky soils.

Potato Bush, Wild Gooseberry *Solanum ellipticum* A spreading greyish plant with short dense hairs on all parts, and a few to a number of prickles on stems, flower stalks and sometimes on leaves. Leaves elliptical to egg shaped, often with wavy edges and purple towards base. Flowers purple with close yellow stamens. Fruit globular, yellowish green often tinged with purple. Occurs on stony and sandy soils. Fruit eaten by Aborigines.

Nicotinia This genus includes the commercial tobacco plant.

Wild Tobacco *Nicotinia occidentalis* An erect plant to 0.5 m. Leaves clustered at base of plant, elliptical to lance shaped with small leaves on flowerstalk. Flowers white tubular with spreading lobes. Occurs on heavy and rocky soils often in shaded positions.

Wild Tobacco *Nicotinia excelsior* An erect plant to 1 m or more. Leaves elliptical to lance shaped mostly at base. Flowers white to yellowish. Occurs in gullies and along creek banks.

Thorn Apple *Datura leichhardtia* Also belonging to the potato family, this erect plant reaches 1 m or more in height. Leaves egg to rhomboid shape with coarse toothed edges. Flowers long, funnel shaped, white. Fruit globular with slender spines. Occurs on various soils on plain areas and along watercourses.

a   Wild Tomato *Solanum quadriloculatum*
b   *Nicotinia occidentalis*
c   Potato Bush *Solanum ellipticum*

Pituri *Duboisia hopwoodii* An erect bushy shrub 2 to 3 m high. Leaves narrow to lance shaped. Flowers bell shaped with 5 spreading lobes, white with purple stripes in throat. Fruit a fleshy berry. Leaves are often chewed by Aborigines. Occurs chiefly on red sandy ridges.

Cattle Bush *Trichodesma zeylanicum* A slender plant 60 cm to 1 m. Leaves lance shaped broad to narrow, soft hairy. Flowers light blue to reddish or white with a short tube and spreading lobes. Occurs on red sandy soil, dunes and rocky hillside.

Hibbertia glaberima An erect bushy shrub 1 to 2 m high. Leaves smooth oblong to elliptical. Flowers bright yellow with 5 spreading petals. Occurs in protected shaded gullies, eg. Kings Canyon.

The Legume Family

This large family includes a number of cultivated vegetables such as peas. These plants all have seed pods or legumes of different shapes which split open and release a number of hard seeds.

Senna These plants have 5 petalled saucer shaped flowers with 5 stamens and a curved style. Leaves are usually divided into a number of leaflets.

Silver Cassia *Senna artemisioides* A bushy shrub to about 3 m. Leaves silvery grey with a number of narrow leaflets. Flowers yellow, showy, in clusters. Occurs on various soils but prefers rocky and sandy types.

Senna nemophila var. *platypoda* Slender erect shrub 1 to 3 m with several different varieties. Leaves green to greyish with 1 to 2 pairs of leaflets, slightly hairy. Flowers yellow in groups of 3 to 10. Occurs chiefly on sandy soils.

Stripe Pod Cassia *Senna pleurocarpa* A bushy shrub to 2 m. Leaves yellowish green with 5 to 9 pairs of leaflets. Flowers yellow in long sprays. Seed pods striped.

Senna helmsii A bushy shrub 0.5 to 1 m. Leaves and stems silvery grey with 3 to 4 pairs of wedge shaped leaflets. Flowers yellow in short spreading heads. Occurs in sandy and rocky type soils.

a

b

c

d

a   Silver Cassia *Senna artemisiodes*
b   *Senna nemophila* var. *platypoda*
c   *Senna pleurocarpa*
d   *Senna helmsii*

Senna venusta

Senna venusta An erect spreading shrub 1 to 2 m. Leaves large greyish green with 6 to 15 pairs of leaflets. Flowers yellow in long sprays. Occurs on sandy and rocky soils.
Senna sturtii A variable shrub 1 to 2 m. Leaves whitish grey, smooth to hairy with 3 to 6 pairs of leaflets. Flowers yellow in groups of 4 to 5. Occurs on various soils.
Cockroach Bush *Senna notabilis* A bushy shrub 0.5 to 1 m. Leaves with a number of hairy leaflets. Occurs mainly on gravelly soils.

Petalostylis Closely allied to *Senna* but flowers have 5 stamens, style is flattened and petal-like. Flowers yellow marked with red at centre.
Petalostylis cassioides A bushy shrub to 1.5 m. Leaves long with 23 to 25 pairs of egg shaped leaflets. Flowers yellow with red centre. Occurs on rocky and sandy soils.

Petalostylis cassioides

Lysophyllum Formerly included with *Bauhinia*.
Lysophyllum gilvum A large bushy shrub to tree to 9 m. Leaves with pairs of egg shaped leaflets. Flowers long red with projecting stamens. Occurs on plain areas on various soils.
Sturt's Desert Pea *Swainsona formosa* A spreading silvery grey plant. Leaves feathery with a number of woolly grey leaflets. Flowers with large bright shiny red keel, standard turned back usually with a purplish-black base. Occurs on various soils.

Lysiphyllum gilvum

Sturt's Desert Pea *Swainsona formosa*

Psoralea This group of pea flowers have leaves with 3 leaflets and sprays of small flowers.

Psoralea cinerea A slender erect plant to about 1 m. Leaves with 3 elliptical pointed leaflets. Flowers small pink to purple, in groups of 3 on long terminal sprays. Occurs on flood plains and areas subject to flooding.

Psoralea australasica Similar to *P. cinerea* but leaflets greyish rhomboid to lance shaped, coarsely toothed.

Swainsona This group of pea flowers contains a number of different species whose leaves have varying numbers of leaflets. Flowers are followed by inflated seed pods.

Broughton Pea *Swainsona procumbens* A variable spreading plant, erect to prostrate, stems with fine white hairs. Leaves long with 17 to 23 greyish green leaflets. Flowers large blue to purple, keel distinctly twisted. Occurs chiefly on sandy soils, widely distributed.

Small Leaf Swainsona *Swainsona microphylla* A spreading plant with variable smooth to hairy leaves with up to 21 small leaflets. Flowers small blue purple, yellow or white. Occurs on various soils from sand plains to heavy clays, widely distributed.

Downy Swainsona *Swainsona swainsonioides* A spreading plant forming small to large clumps. Leaves long and greyish with up to 21 small leaflets. Flowers blue to purple on long spikes. Occurs on clay and loamy soils.

Swainsona canescens A strong growing large plant with hairy stems. Leaves large with 9 to 17 greyish leaflets. Flowers large purple or yellow on long crowded spikes. Occurs on sand plains, widely distributed.

Dwarf Swainsona *Swainsona phacoides* A small spreading plant with erect stems. Leaves greyish with 9 leaflets. Flowers purple, yellow or white in short sprays. Occurs on sandy soils, widely distributed.

Batswing Coral Tree *Erythrina vespertilio* A spreading tree 5 to 12 m with rough corky bark and prickly branches. Leaves divided into 2 batswing like lobes. Flowers red with a short keel and wings, stamens projecting. Occurs along the banks of rocky watercourses on ridges and floodplains.

a   *Psoralea cinerea*
b   Downy Swainsona *Swainsona swainsonioides*
c   Batswing Coral Tree *Erythrina vespertilio*
d   Broughton Pea *Swainsona procumbens*
e   Small Leaf Swainsona *Swainsona microphylla*

a   *Indigofera basedowii*
b   *Glycine canescens*
c   *Crotalaria novaehollandiae*
d   *Crotalaria eremaea*
e   Green Bird Flower *Crotalaria cunninghamii*
f   Wallflower Poison Pea *Cstrolobium grandiflorum*

Indigofera A group of plants with small pea flowers and feathery leaves.
Indigofera basedowii A bushy greyish shrub to 1 m. Leaves with 3 to 21 silvery grey leaflets. Flowers small, red to purple, in short dense sprays. Occurs on rocky hillside and gorges.

Glycine A group of twining plants with small pea flowers and leaves of 3 leaflets.
Glycine canescens A slender twining plant. Leaves with 3 narrow greyish green leaflets. Flowers blue to purple in slender sprays. Occurs on sandy and rocky soil along dry watercourses.

Rattlepods, Crotolaria A group of pea flowers with leaves divided into 3 leaflets or single. The flowers have a somewhat birdlike appearance. Seed pods are inflated and, when dry, rattle with the seeds inside.
Crotalaria eremaea An erect slender shrub to 1 m. Leaves silvery grey with a single leaf or 3 leaflets. Flowers small yellow on long slender sprays. Occurs commonly on dunes and heavy red sandy loam.
Crotalaria novae holandiae An erect bushy shrub to about 1 m. Leaves oblong to egg shaped, greyish green, soft single or with 3 leaflets. Flowers yellow small in dense sprays. Usually occurs on sand dunes.
Green Bird Flower *Crotalaria cunninghamii* A bushy shrub to about 1 m. Leaves fleshy elliptical hairy, single or with 3 leaflets. Flowers greenish yellow large distinctly striped. Occurs on red sand dunes.

Wallflower Poison Pea *Gastrolobium grandiflorum* An erect shrub to about 1 m. Leaves greyish green elliptical. Flowers deep orange, red with brown. This group of pea flowers are poisonous to stock. Occurs in protected gorges in rocky soils along dry watercourses.

a   Mulga *Acacia aneura*
b   Gidgee *Acacia cambagei*
c   Western Myall *Acacia papyrocarpa*
d   Minni Ritchi *Acacia cyperophylla*
e   Ironwood *Acacia estrophiolata*

The Wattles or Acacias

This group of plants belong the legume family and are widely distributed throughout Australia. The more widely distributed types are given common group names such as mulga, gidgee, myall and the like.

Mulgas There are a number of different mulgas, the most common ones being *Acacia aneura* and *A. cyperophylla*.

Acacia aneura A bushy spreading shrub to small tree. Leaves long narrow greyish green. Flowers yellow in rod shaped spikes. Occurs commonly on sand plains, also on rocky soils.

Red Mulga or Minni Ritchie *Acacia cyperophylla* A bushy small spreading tree with the trunk covered in red curly bark. Flowers yellow in rod shaped spikes. Occurs along the banks of rocky dry watercourses.

Gidgees There are several different kinds of gidgee, all of which are large spreading straggly shrubs to trees with rough furrowed bark. Often called stinking wattles, these plants give out an unpleasant odour during wet weather and moist nights and are best avoided when camping. The two common ones, which look much alike, are *Acacia cambagei* and *A. georginae*. Both grow on heavy soils on flood plains of larger river systems.

Acacia cambagei A large spreading shrub or tree with rough furrowed bark. Leaves greyish narrow lance shaped. Flowerheads yellow globular. Occurs on heavy soils on flood plains.

Western Myall *Acacia papyrocarpa* A large shrub to small tree with a dense spreading rounded crown. Leaves long narrow pendulous. Flowers yellow in globular heads. Occurs in the southern part of the area in sandy soils.

Ironwood *Acacia estrophiolata* A large pendulous wattle with rough bark. Leaves long pendulous. Flowerheads pale yellow globular. Occurs on flat sandy areas.

a
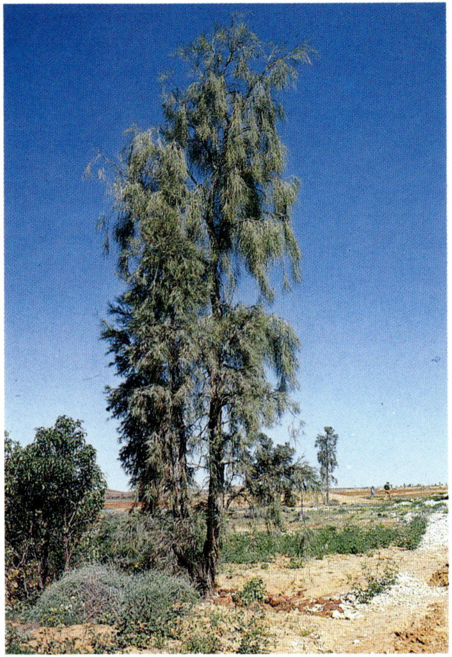
b
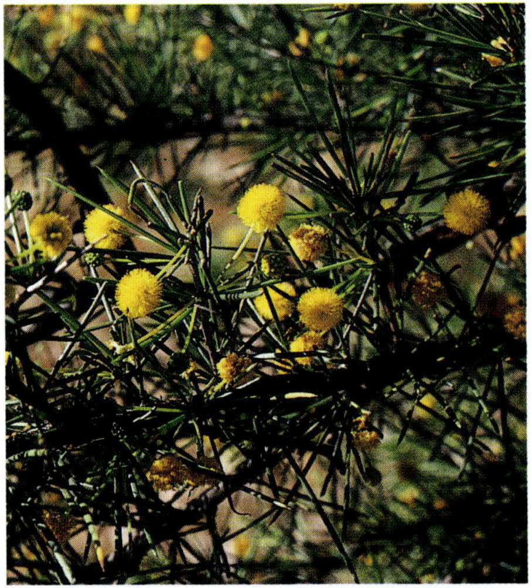
c
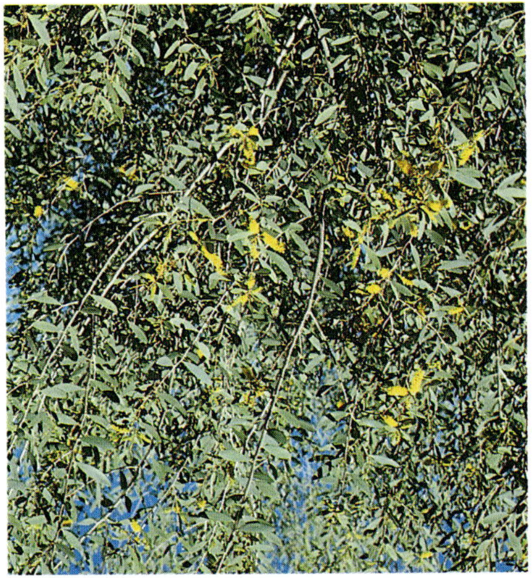
d
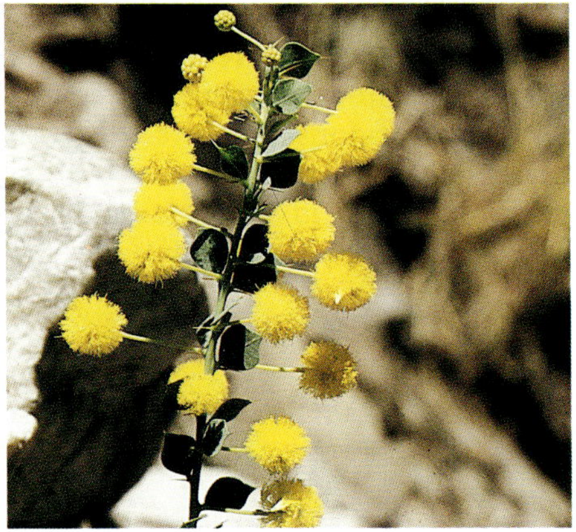
e
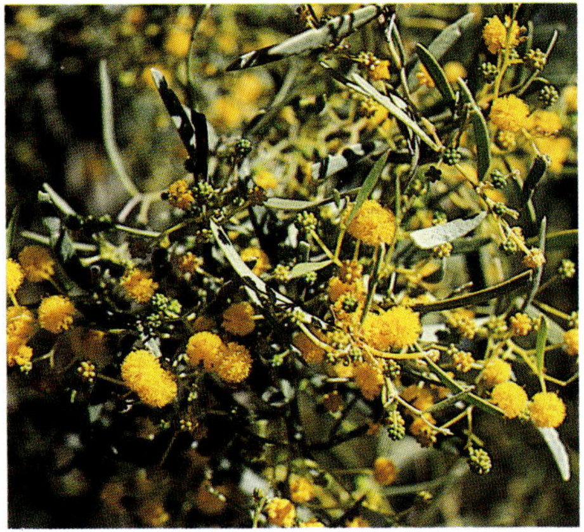

a Waddy Wood *Acacia peuce*
b Dead Finish *Acacia tetragonaphylla*
c Witchetty Bush *Acacia kempeana*
d Round-leaf Wattle *Acacia strongylophylla*
e Dune Wattle *Acacia ligulata*

Waddy Wood *Acacia peuce* A rare unusual wattle resembling a pencil pine to 15 m high. Leaves very long and narrow. Flowers yellow in globular heads. Occurs in sandy soil in a limited section of the northwest area.

Dead Finish *Acacia tetragonophylla* A bushy shrub to small tree. Leaves short narrow stiff and spiny in groups of 4. Flowers yellow in globular heads. Occurs on sandy and rocky soils.

Round Leaf Wattle *Acacia strongylophylla* A bushy shrub 1 to 2 m with sharp spines on the stems. Leaves round to rhomboid with pointed apex. Occurs on stony soils along dry watercourses, eg. Standley Chasm.

Witchetty Bush *Acacia kempeana* A bushy shrub to small tree. Leaves greyish oblong. Flowers yellow in rod shaped spikes. Aborigines obtain witchetty grubs from amongst the roots. Occurs on rocky and sandy soils.

Umbrella or Dune Wattle *Acacia ligulata* A spreading shrub to small tree. Leaves oblong, slightly sickle shaped. Flowers yellow in globular heads. Occurs chiefly on sand dunes.

Maitlands Wattle *Acacia maitlandii* A bushy shrub to 3 m. Leaves small oblong to elliptical, sharply pointed. Flowers golden in globular heads. Occurs on sandy and rocky soils.

Elegant Wattle *Acacia victoriae* A large bushy shrub to tree to 10 m with spines on stems. leaves linear to elliptical. Flowers pale yellow in globular heads. Occurs on various soils, widespread.

Maitlands Wattle *Acacia maitlandii*

The Gum Tree or Eucalypt Family

This family of plants includes the gum trees, paperbarks and a number of other groups which are widely distributed throughout Australia.

The eucalypts There are about 800 different kinds of eucalypts in Australia. The common term gum tree is usually applied to smooth barked species but many of these have a rough base.

Coolibah or Coolabah *Eucalyptus microtheca* A bushy spreading tree with a rough trunk and smooth branches. Leaves greyish green lance shaped. Flowers small white in clusters. This is the tree of the famous song 'Waltzing Matilda'. The plate shows a billabong with a spreading Coolibah tree. Occurs on the banks of watercourses and on flood plains.

River Red Gum *Eucalyptus camaldulensis* A slender to large tree with a trunk to 1 m in diameter. Trunk white to greyish, often with red patches and a rough base. Leaves greyish green lance shaped on pendulous branches. Flowers small white in clusters. Occurs in the

a Coolibah *Eucalyptus microtheca*
b River Gum *Eucalyptus camaldulensis*
c Ghost Gum *Eucalyptus papuana*

beds of rivers such as the Todd and the Finke.

Ghost Gum *Eucalyptus papuana* An erect shapely tree with smooth white powdery surfaced bark. Leaves green pendulous lance shaped. Flowers small white in clusters. Occurs on alluvial and deep soils and on the sides of rocky gorges. This is probably the most photographed of all the eucalypts and is the tree painted so often by the Aboriginal painter Namatjira.

Bloodwood *Eucalyptus terminalis* A spreading tree with rough brown scaly bark. Leaves greyish green lance shaped. Flowers cream in large clusters. Occurs on deep soils and is common around Ayers Rock.

Mallees There are a number of low growing eucalypts with several stems arising from a woody base at ground level. Some of the more common of these are:

Blue Mallee *Eucalyptus gamophylla* A low growing mallee with a number of stems with flaky bark. Leaves grey opposite, joined at base. Flowers small white in clusters. Occurs on sandy soil.

Red Bud Mallee *Eucalyptus pachyphylla* A shrub to mallee to 4 m with a number of pink stems with flaky bark at the base. Leaves thick oval greyish green. Flowers large, covered with a red cap which falls off exposing cream stamens. Occurs on sand plains, particularly Tanami Desert.

Red Mallee *Eucalyptus socialis* A mallee with one to several smooth light grey stems and red branchlets. Leaves narrow lance shaped. Flowers white with a long cap on bud. Occurs on sand plains and dunes.

Paperbarks *Melaleuca* This group of plants have papery bark and fluffy bottlebrush-like flowerheads.

Melaleuca viridiflora A large bushy shrub to tree 3 to 10 m. Bark papery. Leaves broad elliptical. Flowers green in cylindrical spikes. Occurs in the northern part of the area in swampy areas and along creek banks.

Tea Tree *Melaleuca linariifolia* A bushy shrub to 5 m with papery bark. Leaves narrow pointed dark green. Flowers cream in loose cylindrical spikes.

Inland Tea Tree *Melaleuca glomerata* A bushy shrub 1 to 3 m, bark papery. Leaves small narrow pointed. Flowers pale yellow in small globular heads. Occurs in low lying areas subject to flooding.

Melaleuca viridiflora

Calytrix longiflora A spreading shrub 1 to 1.5 m. Leaves small oblong crowded. Flowers pink with 5 long pointed petals and calyx lobes and yellow fluffy stamens; the calyx remains after the petals have fallen. Occurs on sand and gravelly plains and rocky hillsides.

Thryptomene maisonneuvei A bushy twiggy shrub 1 to 1.5 m. Leaves tiny opposite, crowded overlapping. Flowers small white to pink with 5 small rounded spreading petals; there are 5 small stamens between petals. Occurs on red sand dunes and is common on dunes around Ayers Rock.

Micromyrtus flaviflora A straggly shrub to 1.5 m. Leaves tiny narrow crowded. Flowers small pink to yellowish with 5 spreading petals. Differs from *Thryptomene* in stamens being opposite the petals. Occurs in protected gullies in gravelly and sandy soils.

a   *Calytrix longiflora*
b   *Thryptomene maisonneuvei*
c   *Micromyrtus flaviflora*

The Proteaceae Family

The family includes the South African proteas, the New South Wales floral emblem the Waratah, *Telopea speciosissima*, and many other interesting plants. The flowers differ from most flowers in having no separate petals and calyx, with a number of flowers grouped into clusters or spikes.

Grevillea There are over 250 different grevilleas in Australia. The flowers have conspicuous styles and are rich in nectar. The seed case with the old style attached contains 2 seeds.

Grevillea juncifolia A bushy shrub to 3 m. Branches and leaves very finely woolly. Leaves long narrow dark green often divided into 5 narrow segments. Flowers golden orange in dense sprays. Occurs on red sand dunes and on swales between dunes.

Grevillea eriostachya Similar to *G. juncifolia*, but leaves are divided into 7 segments, flower spikes are one sided, and the sticky style is slightly shorter. Occurs in similar locations to *G. juncifolia*.

Grevillea stenobotrya An erect bushy shrub to 2 m. Leaves long and narrow.

Grevillea juncifolia

Grevillea stenobotrya

Grevillea wickhamii

Beefwood *Grevillea striata*

Flowers white to cream in long dense erect spikes. Occurs on red sand dunes and in swales between dunes.

Grevillea wickhamii A bushy spreading shrub 2 to 3 m. Leaves grey round and holly-like. Flowers bright red in pendulous or erect clusters. Occurs on rocky soils, hillsides and dunes.

Beefwood *Grevillea striata* A small bushy tree to 9 m with grey furrowed bark. Leaves very long and narrow. Flowers cream in dense spikes. Occurs on sand plains, loamy and gravelly soils.

Hakea This group of plants is closely allied to *Grevillea* but differs in the woody fruit with 2 winged seeds.

Corkwood *Hakea chordophylla* A small tree 3 to 7 m with deeply furrowed corky bark. Branchlets and leaves without hairs. Leaves very long to 9 cm, tough cylindrical sharply pointed. Flowers cream to yellow in long dense smooth sprays. Occurs on sand plains.

Needlewood *Hakea leucoptera* A large bushy shrub to small tree to about 7 m. Leaves needle like to 9 cm long. Flowers white in dense sprays; fruit numerous woody egg shaped. Occurs on sandy loam in low lying areas and along creeks.

Hakea eyreana   A bushy shrub or small tree to 7 m. Leaves greyish green forked, needle-like with sharp lobes. Flowers cream to yellow in dense sprays. Woody fruit tapered to apex. Occurs on low lying flats and creek beds.

Corkwood *Hakea lorea*   A small tree 3 to 7 m with grey furrowed bark. Leaves needle-like, long to 30 cm, new growth woolly. Flowers cream in dense spikes. Close to *H. chordophylla*, differing chiefly in woolly flowers and new growth. Occurs on sand plains.

a   Corkbark Tree *Hakea chordophylla*
b   *Hakea eyreana*
c   Needlewood *Hakea leucoptera*
d   Corkbark Tree *Hakea lorea*

White Cypress Pine *Callitris glaucophylla* An erect symmetrical tree 4 to 8 m. Foliage greyish to dark green. Fruit cones globular. Occurs on rocky hillsides.

Wild Orange *Capparis mitchellii* A large bushy shrub to 3 m. Leaves thick elliptical. Flowers white to yellow with pincushion-like styles. Fruit round 5 to 7 cm diameter on a long stalk.

a White Cypress Pine *Callitris glaucophylla*
b Wild Orange *Capparis mitchellii*
c Desert Oak *Alocasuarina decaisneana*
d Capparis species

The Mistletoes, Quandongs and Other Parasitic Plants

This group of plants attach themselves to other plants and make use of their nutrients. Their leaves often resemble those of the host plant.

Mistletoes These grow on the bark of other plants which they penetrate so as to make use of the sap.

Lysiana casuarinae A parasitic plant with cylindrical leaves. Flowers usually in pairs or single, tubular, red with 6 green lobes. Fruit fleshy ovoid shape. Occurs chiefly on *Allocasuarina* and *Acacia* species.

Lysiana subfalcata A parasitic plant. Leaves broad lance shaped. Flowers tubular, red with yellow to green apex, dividing into 6 lobes. Fruit fleshy ellipsoid. Occurs on various plants such as *Acacia, Allocasuarina, Atalaya, Santalum*

a Mistletoe *Lysiana casuarinae*
b Mistletoe *Lysiana subfalcata*

Mistletoe *Amyema gibberulum*

Lysiana spathulata A parasitic plant. Similar to *L. subfalcata* but leaves spoon shaped, rounded at apex and fruit with a small nipple at apex. Occurs on *Ficus, Acacia, Eucalyptus,* and *Melaleuca.*

Amyema Differs from *Lysiana* in the flowers which occur in twos and threes and divide into 4 or 6 lobes which split to the base.

Amyema gibberulum A woolly parasitic plant. Leaves narrow cylindrical greyish woolly. Flowers red with 4 lobes. Occurs only on *Hakea* and *Grevillea.*

Quandongs These parasitic plants attach themselves to the roots of other plants and grow into small trees 6 m high. They have tiny tubular flowers, fruit with a fleshy covering and a woody wrinkled seed case, which has been used in the game Chinese checkers. The wood is processed as sandalwood and is also used in eastern countries as incense.

Quandong *Santalum acuminatum* A busy shrub to small tree 6 m. Leaves narrow lance shaped on pendulous branchlets. Flowers tiny greenish yellow. Fruit bright shiny red when ripe, 2 to 2.5 cm diameter. Occurs on sandy and loamy soils amongst shrubs.

Plum Bush *Santalum lanceolatum* A bushy shrub to small tree 7 m. Leaves broad lance shaped. Flowers tiny cream to pale green. Fruit globular, brownish to purplish with a round scar at apex. Occurs on flat areas, banks of creeks and gullies, in woodland around Ayers Rock.

Broom Rape *Orobanche cernua* var. *australasiana* An unusual fleshy parasitic plant without green leaves. Stem stout and fleshy with small triangular bracts. Flowers tubular, lobed at apex, pinkish purple. Occurs in dry creek beds.

a   Quandong *Santalum acuminatum*
b   Australian Broom Rape *Orobanche cernua* var. *australiana*
c   Plum Bush *Santalum lanceolatum*

The Myoporum Family

Myoporum This group of shrubs to small trees have fleshy leaves and small tubular flowers with 5 spreading lobes, round to flattened fruit.
Native Myrtle *Myoporum acuminatum* A bushy shrub 1 to 2 m. Leaves lance shaped fleshy light green. Flowers white small bell shaped. Fruit globular white to reddish purple. Occurs on sandy and rocky soils.
Sugar Wood *Myoporum platycarpum* A large shrub to small tree 10 m. Leaves light green lance shaped. Flowers bell shaped white. Fruit flattened. A sugary resinous sap is exuded on the branches. Occurs on sandy and rocky soils in southern part of the area.

Emu Bush, *Eremophila* This group of shrubs to small trees have tubular lobed flowers followed by hard fruit with a fleshy surface. The calyx remains after the petals have fallen, often enlarging and becoming coloured.
Eremophila duttonii A bushy shrub 1 to 3 m. Leaves lance shaped. Flowers red often marked with yellow, stamens projecting, calyx enlarges and becomes coloured. Occurs on various types of soils.
Eremophila latrobei An open shrub 1 to 3 m. Flowers purplish pink to red, often with yellow inside. Occurs on various types of soils.
Native Fuchsia *Eremophila maculata* A spreading to erect shrub 1 to 1.5 m. Leaves lance shaped narrow to broad. Flowers red or yellow, inner surface distinctly spotted, lower lip rolled back. Occurs on a wide range of soils.
Eremophila christopheri An erect shrub to 2 m. Leaves elliptical crowded. Flowers blue neatly arranged. Occurs chiefly on rocky soils.
Eremophila freelingii A large spreading bushy shrub. Leaves long greyish green soft, somewhat sticky. Flowers pale blue. Occurs chiefly on rocky soils.

a Native Myrtle *Myoporum acuminatum*
b *Eremophila duttonii*
c *Eremophila christopheri*
d *Eremophila latrobei*
e Native Fuchsia *Eremophila maculata*
f *Eremophila freelingii*

Palms and Palm-like Plants

There is one native palm in the area, *Livistona mariae* confined to Palm Valley. Throughout the area there are a number of exotic Date Palms which have been planted since the early days of settlement; their leaves are feather shaped. The other low growing plant which looks like a palm is the cycad *Macrozamia macdonnellii*. Both native plants are relic plants, being remnants of vegetation which existed in Central Australia millions of years ago when the climate was more equable. At present they survive only in protected valleys where there is constant moisture.

Cabbage or Maria Palm *Livistona mariae* A tall palm to about 20 m with a rough trunk. The large fan shaped leaves have a long spiny stalk. Flowers tiny yellowish green, produced in large numbers on much branched sprays amongst the leaves. Fruit globular, black when ripe. Occurs only on the Finke River and its tributaries where there is constant moisture. Recent work has shown that this palm is very closely related to the Cabbage Palm at Mataranka south of Darwin.

Macrozamia macdonnelli Commonly known as a cycad, this plant with the trunk mostly below the ground has large dark green leaves about 2 m long with the leaflets crowded along the stalk which has a sharp pointed apex. These plants do not produce flowers but have large male or female cones at the top of the plant. The female cones develop and produce large seeds. Occurs only in protected gullies of the Macdonnell Ranges where there is adequate moisture and shade for most of the day.

Top right: Cycad *Macrozamia macdonnellii*
Bottom: Cabbage Palm *Livistona mariae*

Berrigan *Pittosporum phylliraeoides* A tree to 10 m with rough grey bark and pendulous branches. Flowers small yellow bell shaped. Fruit globular yellow to orange. Occurs on low lying areas in loamy soil and in creek beds.

Grue, Sour Apple *Owenia acidula* A large bushy shrub to small spreading tree. Leaves long with a number of 10 to 25 lance shaped leaflets. Flowers small brownish white, in sprays. Fruit globular 2 cm diameter with a red fleshy outer coating. Occurs on red sands and dunes.

Desert Walnut *Owena reticulata* Similar to *O. acidula* but leaves covered with a yellow sticky substance, leaflets narrower 4 to 12. Fruit pear shaped red to purplish. Occurs on sand plains amongst spinifex.

Desert poplar *Codonocarpus cotinfolius* An erect bushy short lived tree to 10 m. Leaves egg to broad lance shaped. Male and female flowers on separate plants. Flowers without petals in lobed circular rings, fruit bell shaped. Occurs on red sand loam and dunes.

Fig *Ficus platypoda* A spreading shrub on rock faces to small bushy tree. Leaves lance shaped, green above greyish beneath. Flowers minute followed by round orange to red fleshy fruit. Occurs in gullies on rock outcrops and rock faces including Ayers Rock.

Whitewood *Atalaya hemiglauca* A large bushy shrub to small tree 5 m. Leaves greyish with 2 to 6 pairs of smooth leaflets. Flowers small in slender sprays. Occurs on sandy soil in woodland.

a Desert Poplar *Codonocarpus cotinifolius*
b Berrigan *Pittosporum phylliraeoides*
c *Ficus platypoda*
d Gruie, Sour Apple *Owenia acidula*

The Mint Bush Family

Plectanthus intraterraneus An erect shrub to 1 m with square stems. Leaves greyish green egg shaped fleshy aromatic. Flowers distinctly lipped, violet. Occurs in rocky gullies and creek beds.

Teucrium racemosum An erect plant to about 1 m with 4-angled stems. Leaves narrow egg to elliptical shaped. Flowers bell shaped, in lower part white with a broad lower lip, in slender sprays. Occurs on heavy clay soils.

Mint Bush *Prostanthera striatiflora* A bushy shrub to 2 m. Leaves light green aromatic lance shaped. Flowers white bell shaped, distinctly 2-lipped with purple striping and yellow markings in throat. Occurs in shaded gullies in sandy soils.

Rostellaria pogonanthera An erect plant with a number of stems to 40 cm. Leaves soft hairy elliptical. Flowers small bell shaped, pink to purple in dense spikes. Occurs on sandy soils, alluvials, clays and gibber plains.

Spearwood Bush *Pandorea dorotoxylon* A scrambling shrub with a number of flexible stems to about 4 m. Leaves greyish green smooth, with 3 to 5 long narrow leaflets. Flowers bell shaped, cream with brown markings on throat. Occurs in protected gullies eg. The Olgas, Kings Canyon.

a   *Plectranthus intraterraneus*
b   *Teucrium racemosum*
c   *Rostellaria pogonanthera*
d   Mint Bush *Prostanthera striatiflora*

Mimulus repens A prostrate mat forming plant. Leaves small soft egg shaped. Flowers tubular 2-lipped blue, mauve or pink. Occurs on areas subject to flooding on edges of swamps and dry watercourses.

Blue Rod *Stemodia glabra* A small plant to about 35 cm with several stems. Leaves narrow lance shaped fleshy aromatic. Flowers bell shaped 2-lipped with 2 white steaks on lower lip. Occur son clay pans and depressed areas.

Stemodia floribunda Similar to *S. glabra* but without white streaks on lower lip.

Stemodia viscosa An erect bushy plant to 80 cm. Leaves egg shaped to elliptical, sticky. Flowers purple 2-lipped. Occurs in protected shaded areas on creek riverbeds and banks of waterholes.

Clerodendron floribundum A large bushy shrub to small tree. Leaves elliptical. Flowers white tubular lipped. Fruit with purplish seeds and enlarged fleshy red calyx lobes. Occurs on heavier soils with ample moisture.

a *Clerodendrum floribundum*
b *Mimulus repens*
c Blue Rod *Stemodia glabra*

Blue Bell *Wahlenbergia communis* A small plant with several slender stems. Leaves narrow to elliptical, slightly hairy. Flowers bell shaped, blue sometimes white. Occurs chiefly on sandy loams.
Wahlenbergia gracilis Similar to *W. communis* but generally smaller
Rock Isotoma *Isotoma petraea* A small plant with a number of slender branched stems. Leaves coarsely toothed or lobed. Flowers tubular blue to white with 5 spreading lobes. Care should be taken in handling these plants as the milky sap will burn the eyes if it is transferred from the hands. Occurs on rocky hillsides in rock crevices.

a   Bluebell *Wahlenbergia gracilis*
b   Rock Isotoma *Isotoma petraea*

The Goodenia Family

There are a number of different groups and species in this family, all of which are herbaceous plants.

Goodenia grandiflora A spreading plant with round to egg shaped coarsely toothed sticky leaves. Flowers tubular with 5 one sided spreading lobes, white to pale blue with purple striping. Occurs in rock crevices in protected gullies.

Goodenia pinnatifida A variable spreading plant to 8 cm. Leaves oblong to broad lance shaped, lobed or coarsely toothed. Flowers yellow tubular, with 5 lobes, 2 erect 3 spreading. Occurs on sand dunes and sandy soils.

Scaevola ovalifolia A spreading plant to 6 cm. Leaves oblong to round, hairy. Flowers pale blue with 5 spreading one sided lobes. Occurs on sandy and stony soils.

Scaevola depauperata A spreading shrub to about 60 cm. Leaves narrow to lance shaped. Flowers blue to cream with 5 spreading one sided lobes. Occurs on sand dunes.

a *Goodenia grandiflora*
b *Goodenia* species
c *Scaevola ovalifolia*

Blue Pincushion *Brunonia australis* A small tufted plant with soft lance shaped leaves at ground level. Flowers small tubular with spreading lobes with a number grouped into a dense globular head. Occurs chiefly on sandy soils.

Snow flower *Macgregoria racemigera* A compact plant 3 to 15 cm. Leaves small narrow. Flowers white with 5 petals in slender sprays above leaves forming a dense floral mass. Occurs on red sandy soil, sandy loam and stony soil, often in depressions.

a Blue Pincushion *Brunonia australis*
b Snow Flower *Macgregoria racemigera*

Keraudrenia integrifolia

Rulingia magniflora

Frankenia cordata

The Kurrajong Family

This group of plants includes the east coast rainforest tree, the Flame Tree *Brachychiton acerifolius*.

Keraudrenia integrifolia   A bushy shrub to about 1 m. Leaves oblong, green above greyish below. Flowers violet to blue with 5 spreading petal-like lobes. Occurs on red sandy soils and rocky hillsides.

Rulingia magniflora   A bushy shrub to 2 m. Leaves oblong to lance shaped, woolly velvety, shallowly toothed. Flowers pink with 5 spreading petal-like lobes. Occurs in protected shaded gorges, eg. Kings Canyon.

Desert Poplar *Brachychiton gregorii*   A small tree with a compact crown. Leaves divided into 3 to 5 pointed lobes. Flowers bell shaped, cream with red. Occurs chiefly on sand dunes.

Frankenia cordata   A small spreading to clump-forming plant with small, heart-shaped to egg-shaped leaves; flowers pink, 6-petalled. Occurs around the margins of saltpans, salt lakes and in saline soils.

The Salt Bush Group

The plants of this group are able to grow in soils with a high salt content which they are able to excrete through the leaves.

Salt Bush *Atriplex mummularia* A bushy plant 1 to 2 m. Leaves soft grey fleshy. Flowers separate male or female, cream male small in clusters, female flowers without petals but with 2 petal-like bracteoles. Fruit with a mebranous wing surrounding a hard seed. Occurs on various saline soils.

Pop Saltbush *Atriplex holocarpa* A spreading plant to 30 cm. Leaves grey fleshy oval. Fruit cream to red, round and spongy and pops when pressed tightly. Occurs on various types of soils.

Frankenia cordata A spreading mat forming plant. Leaves small heart shaped. Flowers pink 4 to 6 petals. Occurs around the margins of saltpans.

Rhagodia nutans (now *Einadia nutans*) A spreading plant with a number of branched stems. Leaves narrow heart shaped grey fleshy. Flowers tiny cream. Fruit round red shiny fleshy. Occurs on various soils.

a   Saltbush *Atriplex*
b   Saltbush *Rhagodia nutans*
c   Pop Saltbush *Atriplex holocarpa*

Ruby Salt Bush *Enchyleana tomentosa* A spreading shrub. Leaves cylindrical fleshy. Flowers tiny cream. Fruit shiny red fleshy berry. Occurs on various soils.

Cannon Ball *Dissocarpus paradoxa* A spreading plant. Leaves narrow greyish fleshy. Flowers small cream followed by woolly looking fruit which cover sharp spines. These fruit fall to the ground where they can remain for indefinite periods, presenting problems for persons camping in such areas and possibly making an area unsuitable for camping. Occurs chiefly on hard stony soils.

Samphire *Halosarcia Pruinosa* An erect plant with numerous fleshy almost leafless jointed stems. Flowers tiny cream followed by small spongy fruit.

Blue Bush *Maireana sedifolia* A straggling plant to about 1 m. Leaves narrow fleshy greyish. Flowers tiny cream followed by yellow winged membranous fruit. Occurs on calcareous soils in the southern part of the area.

Copper Burr *Sclerolaena limbata* A spreading plant. Leaves narrow fleshy hoary. Flowers tiny followed by woolly fruit covering several long hard sharp spines. These fall to the ground and make camping almost impossible. Occurs on hard stony type soils.

Blue Bush *Maireana georgei* An open shrub to 1 m. Leaves narrow angular fleshy bluish grey. Flowers small cream, followed by winged membranous red mottled fruit. Occurs chiefly on calcareous soils.

Lignum *Muehlenbeckia cunninghamii* A stiff spreading shrub 2 to 4 m with numerous tough branching almost leafless spiny stems forming dense clumps. Flowers tiny cream. Occurs on low lying heavy soils subject to flooding and along the banks of watercourses. In some flood areas it forms an impenetrable mass.

a Ruby Saltbush *Enchylaena tomentosa*
b Bluebush *Maireana sedifolia*
c Cannon Ball *Dissocarpus paradoxa*
d Lignum *Meuhlenbeckia cunninghamii*
e Bluebush *Maireana georgei*
f Copper Burr *Sclerolaena limbata*
g Samphire *Haloscarcia pruinosa*

Hop Bush, *Dodonaea* There are a number of different kinds of these plants which have small flowers followed by winged fruits resembling hops.

Hop Bush *Dodonaea lanceolata* An erect shrub 1 to 2 m. Leaves elliptical to broad lance shaped with thickened edges. Flowers tiny cream. Fruit 3 winged reddish. Occurs in open woodland on rocky hillsides and along watercourses.

Hop Bush *Dodonaea petiolaris* An erect shrub 1 to 3 m. Leaves smooth sticky, broad lance shaped to egg shaped. Flowers tiny. Fruit large 3-winged much inflated mottled pink. Occurs on gibber plains, rocky hills and amongst mulga.

Hop Bush *Dodonaea viscosa var. spathulata* A bushy shrub 1 to 2 m. Leaves spatula shaped with a broad pointed top. Flowers tiny. Fruit 3 to 4-winged but not inflated, mottled pink. Occurs on rocky hilly areas.

Bullhead *Tribulus occidentalis* A spreading mat forming plant. Leaves soft grey with a number of grey hairy leaflets. Flowers large with 5 soft buttercup yellow petals. Fruit with long hard sharp spines. This innocent looking plant is a trap for the unwary photographer who, on kneeling or placing hands on the ground, finds the skin penetrated by the sharp spines. Occurs on sand, sand dunes and stony soils.

Clasping Twin leaf *Zygophyllum howittii* A spreading clump forming plant. Leaves fleshy, lobed at the apex. Flowers small yellow with 3 petals. Fruit 3-winged fleshy reddish purple. Occurs on sand dunes and rocky soils.

a   Hopbush *Dodonaea lanceolata*
b   Hopbush *Dodonaea viscosa*
c   Hopbush *Dononaea petiolaris*
d   Clasping Twin-leaf *Zygophyllum howittii*
e   Bullhead *Tribulus occidentalis*

Ferns

Rock Ferns, *Cheilanthes* These small ferns which grow in the crevices of rocks, eg. Ayers Rock and the Olgas, are unusual in that they die down during dry periods and remain in a brown dead looking state until rain comes; then within a few days they begin to grow again. This process is repeated indefinitely.

Rock Fern *Cheilanthes tenuifolia* A small fern to about 15 cm with coarse small green fronds. Occurs in the crevices of rocks.

Woolly Cloak Fern *Cheilanthes lasiophylla* A small fern to about 15 cm with small woolly brown fronds.

Nardoo, *Marsillea* This unusual group of ferns with 4-lobed fronds resembling a 4-leaved clover have spores in seed-like cases and grow in depressions subject to flooding and in waterholes where the fronds float on the surface. When the water dries up these plants die down and remain in this state until more rain comes when they begin to grow again. There are 4 different kinds in the area, the more common being:

**Common Nardoo *Marsillea drummon-*

dii An extensively creeping plant with numerous slender stalks with greyish softly hairy to smooth leaflets. Occurs in depressions subject to flooding.

Nardoo *Marsillea mutica* This plant is commonly found floating on the surface of pools such as in Ormiston Gorge. The leaflets have a yellowish green central portion.

a Rock Fern *Cheilanthes tenuifolia*
b Nardoo *Marsilea hirsuta*
c Buffel Grass *Cenchrus ciliaris*
d Kangaroo Grass *Themeda australis*

Nardoo *Marsillea hirsuta* This species with creeping stems has the leaflets widely spaced with scalloped edges. Occurs in areas where water remains for a period as a small pond.

Grasses

There are many different grasses in the area including a number of introduced naturalised species. There are two main groups, those which grow as tufted plants and those which grow as tussocks or mounds. As well as having sharp leaves, a number of grasses have seed with sharp bristles, awns or barbs and often a sharp point which enables the seed to penetrate the ground. For the person walking through the grass discomfort is often felt when the seeds penetrate the socks and clothing and work their way into the skin.

Buffel Grass *Cenchrus ciliaris* A strong grass which forms large tufts. Occurs commonly around Ayers Rock amongst Bloodwood trees. This is an introduced species from the Americas.

Themeda australis A tall leafy tufted grass forming large tufts to 90 cm or more with loose seedheads. Seed has a long bent extension. Occurs chiefly in protected areas along banks of creeks.

Flinders Grass, *Iseilema* There are several different kinds of these grasses which are tufted, usually reddish coloured and form close dense seed-

heads. The plate shows budgerigars feeding on the grass seed. These grasses occur on heavy cracking types of clay and alluvial soils, often with Mitchell grass.

Aristida This group of grasses have various common names and have seed with a sharp pointed base and a 3-awned bristly apex. Two common widespread species are *A. latifolia*, Feathertop Wire

a Flinders Grass *Iseilema* species
b Mitchell Grass *Astrebla pectinata*
c Erect Kerosene Grass *Aristida browniana*
d Bristly Love Grass *Eragrostis setifolia*

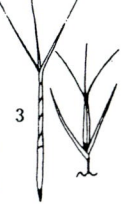

1. Speargrass seed
2. Nine Awn seed
3. Three Awn seed

Grass and *A. contorta*, Sand Spear Grass or Bunched Kerosene Grass.

Erect Kerosene Grass *Aristida browniana* A stiff tufted grass with a seedhead of 3-awned seed. Occurs on river fronts in coarse sandy soil.

Mitchel Grass, *Astrebla* These leafy tufted grasses have a densely packed seedhead on a long stem. There are several different kinds of Mitchell grass. Mitchell Grass *Astrebla pectinata* A leafy tufted grass with the seeds on the head arranged in a dense comb-like manner. Occurs on heavy soil, particularly flood plains.

Love Grass, *Eragrostis* A widespread group of grasses from small tufted types to tall growing forms. The seedheads are closely packed flattened spikelets.
Bristly Love Grass *Eragrostis setifolia* A large leafy grass to about 1 m. Seed in a flattened spikelet. Occurs on sandy soils subject to flooding.

Nine Awn Grass, *Enneapogon* Tufted grasses usually with hairy leaves. Seedheads are compact; seeds have 9 projecting awns. Widespread in the area.

Cane Grass *Zygochloa paradoxa* A tall robust grass with thick stems to 1.5 cm high, forming tangled tussocks. Seedheads in clusters. Common on sand dunes particularly the Simpson Desert.

Hummock grasses The common name of spinifex is given to two groups of grasses, *Triodia* and *Plectrachne*, which form mounds or hummocks with bare areas between the clumps. The largest group is *Triodia*. Both groups look much alike, *Plectrachne* differing in the more open growth of the seedhead, the longer extension of the seed case and the 3 distinct awns on the seed. In these grasses the stems repeatedly branch in an outward direction rooting where they touch the ground; they may form large hummocks. In older plants the centre may die and the outer growth forms a distinct ring. Both groups have sharp spiny leaves in groups of 3.

Lobed Spinifex *Triodia basedowii* A compact to straggling hummock grass 20 to 30 cm high, 75 cm wide, sometimes forming rings 1 to 2 m across. Wide-

Cane Grass
Zygochloa paradoxa

a Lobed Spinifex *Triodia basedowii*
b Porcupine Grass *Triodia irritans*
c Gummy Spinifex *Triodia pungens*
d Feathertop Spinifex *Plectrachne schinzii*

dense tussock forming grass 30 cm high and 90 cm across. Seedheads on stems to 1 m. Occurs on sand dunes in the southern part of the area.

Introduced Weeds

Rosy Dock *Rumex vesicarius* This introduced weed is spreading rapidly through the area. An erect plant with fleshy stems and leaves. Flowers in sprays with the pink perianth inflated, enclosing the seed. From Africa and western Asia. Widespread particularly after winter rains. Sometimes called 'native hop'.

Paddy melons There are several members of the cucumber family from Africa and Asia which have become naturalised in the area and grow as spreading plants with lobed leaves, yellow flowers and ovoid to subglobular melon fruit. Two of these are the Paddy Melon *Cucumis myriocarpus* with melons 2 to 2.5 cm in diameter, and the Ulcardo Melon *Cucumis melo* with melons 1.5 to 4 cm long.

spread on sand plains and sandy areas. **Gummy Spinifex** *Triodia pungens* A compact hummock about 60 cm high and wide. Occurs on sandplains, eg. Tanami Desert.
Porcupine Grass *Triodia irritans* A compact grass forming hummocks 60 cm high and 1 m wide. Occurs chiefly on rocky slopes. Plate shows the Olgas in the background with Ayers Rock in the distance on left.
Silvery Spinifex *Plectrachne schinzii* A

Index

Abutilon
  fraseri, 7
  leucopetalum, 7, pl **7**
Acacia
  aneura, 28, pl **28**
  cambagei, 28, pl **29**
  cyperophylla, 28, pl **29**
  estrophiolata, 28, pl **29**
  georginae, 29
  kempeana, 30, pl **31**
  ligulata, 31, pl **30**
  maitlandlandii, 31, pl **30**
  peuce, 31, pl **30**
  strongylophylla, 31, pl **30**
  tetragonaphylla, 31, pl **30**
  victoriae, 31
Achryanthes aspera, 17, pl **16**
Alocasuarina decaisneana, 38, pl **38**
Amyema gibberulum, 40, pl **40**
Aristida
  browniana, 62, pl **62**
  contorta, 62
  latifolia, 61
Astrebla pectinata, 62, pl **61**
Atriplex
  holocarpa, 55, pl **55**
  mummularia, 55, pl **55**
Berrigan, 46, pl **47**
Blennodia canescens, 18, pl **18**
Blue
  Bell, 51, pl **51**
  Pincushion, 53, pl **53**
  Rod, 50, pl **50**
Bogan Flea, 10
Brachychiton gregorii, 54
Brachycome
  ciliaris, 8
  iberidifolia, 8, pl **19**
Brunonia australis, 53, pl **53**
Broom Rape, 40, pl **40**
Bullhead, 58, pl **59**
Bush
  Apple, 12, pl **14**
  Blue-, 56, pl **57**
  Cattle, 20, pl **20**
  Cockroach, 22
  Emu, 42
  Hop, 55, pl **59**
  Pop salt; 55, pl **55**
  Ruby Salt; 55, pl **55**
  Thorn, 22
  Witchety, 31, pl **30**
Cabbage Palm, 45, pl **45**
Calandrinia
  balonensis, 15, pl **15**
  remota, 15, pl **15**

Callitris glaucophylla, 38, pl **38**
Calocephalus platycephalus, 12, pl **14**
Calotis
  cuneifolia, 8
  hispidula, 10
Calytrix longiflora, 34, pl **34**
Cannonballs, 56, pl **57**
Capparis mitchellii, 38, pl **38**
Cassia
  artemisioides, 21, pl **21**
  helmsii, 21, pl **21**
  nemophila, 21, pl **22**
  notabilis, 22
  pleurocarpa, 21, pl **21**
  sturtii, 22
  venusta, 22, pl **22**
Cenchrus ciliaris, 61, pl **60**
Cephalipterum drummondii, 12, pl **13**
Clasping Twin Leaf, 58, pl **59**
Clerodendron floribundum, 50, pl **50**
Clianthus formosus, 23, pl **23**
Copper Burr, 56, pl **57**
Coolibah, 32, pl **32**
Craspedia chrysantha, 12, pl **14**
Crotalaria
  cunninghamii, 27, pl **26**
  eremaea, 27, pl **26**
  novaehollandiae, 27, pl **26**
Cucumis
  melo, 63
  myriocarpus, 63
Daisies
  Bush, 10
  Button, 12
  Blue Burr, 8
  Minnie, 10, **pl 11**
  Pink Everlasting, 10, pl **12**
  Variable Groundsel, 8, pl **19**
  Yellow Everlasting, 10, pl **12**
  Yellow Top, 8, pl **9-10**
  Yellow Top Tall, 8
Desert
  Oak, 38, pl **38**
  Poplar, 46
  Walnut, 46
Dissocarpus paradoxa, 56, pl **57**
Dodonaea
  lanceolata, 58, pl **59**
  petiolaris, 58, pl **59**
  viscosa, 58, pl **59**
Duboisia hopwoodii, 20, pl **20**
Enchylaena tomentosa, 56, pl **57**
Enneapogon, 62, pl **61**
Eragrostis setifolia, 62, pl **61**
Eremophila
  christopheri, 42, pl **43**

  duttonii, 42, pl **43**
  freelingii, 42, pl **43**
  latrobei, 42, pl **43**
  maculata, 42, pl **43**
Erodium cygnorum, 8, pl **11**
Erythrina vespertilio, 24, pl **25**
Eucalyptus
  camaldulensis, 32, pl **32**
  gamophylla, 32
  microtheca, 33, pl **32**
  pachyphylla, 33
  papuana, 33, pl **33**
  socialis, 33
  terminalis, 33
Fern
  Rock, 60, pl **60**
  Woolly Cloak, 60, pl **60**
Ficus platypoda, 46, pl **47**
Fig, 46, pl **47**
Flower
  Snow, 53, pl **53**
  Wall, 27, pl **26**
Frankenia cordata, 54, pl **54**
Fuzzweed, 10
Gastrolobium grandiflorum, 27, pl **26**
Gidgee, 29, pl **28**
Glycine canescens, 27, pl **26**
Goodenia
  grandiflora, 52, pl **52**
  pinnatidifida, 52
Grass
  Buffel, 62, pl **62**
  Flinders, pl **61**
  Kangaroo, 61, pl **60**
  Kerosene, 61, pl **61**
  Love, 62, pl **61**
  Mitchell, 62, pl **61**
  Porcupine, 63, pl **63**
Grevillea
  eriostachya, 35
  juncifolia, 35, pl **35**
  stenobotrya, 35, pl **35**
Grey Wrinklewort, 12
Gum
  Ghost, 33, pl **32**
  River Red, 32, pl **32**
Hakea
  chordophylla, 36, pl **37**
  eyreana, 37, pl **37**
  leusoptera, 36, pl **37**
  suberea, 37, pl **37**
Haloscarcia pruinosa, 56, pl **57**
Helichrysum
  apiculatum, 10, pl **11**
  bracteatum, 10, pl **11**
  cassinianum, 10, pl **11**
Helipterum
  floribunda, 12, pl **13**
  moschatum, 12

  stipitatum, 12
Hibbertia glaberima, 20, pl **20**
Hibiscus sturtii, 6, pl **6**
Indgofera basedowii, 27, pl **26**
Isotoma
  petraea, 51, pl **51**
  Rock, 51, pl **51**
Keraurinia integrifolia, 54, pl **54**
Lavatera plebeia, 6
Lignum, 56, pl **57**
Livistona mariae, 44, pl **45**
Lysiana
  casuarinae, 39, pl **39**
  spathulata, 40
  subfalcata, 39, pl **39**
Lysophyllum gilvum, 22, pl **22**
Macgregoria racemigera, 53, pl **53**
Macrozamia macdonnellii, 44, pl **45**
Maireana
  georgei, 46, pl **47**
  sedifolia, 56, pl **57**
Mallee
  Blue, 33
  Red, 33
  Red Bud, 33
Marsilea
  drummondii, 60
  hirsuta, 60, pl **60**
  mutica, 60
Melaleuca
  glomerata, 33
  linarifolia, 33
  viridiflora, 32, pl **33**
Melon
  Paddy, 63
  Ulcardo, 63
Micromyrtus flaviflora, 34, pl **34**
Mimulus repens, 50, pl **53**
Minuria leptophylla, 10, pl **11**
Muehlenbeckia cunninghamii, 56, pl **57**
Mulga, 28, pl **29**
Myoporum
  acuminatum, 42, pl **43**
  platycarpum, 43
Myriocephalus stuartii, 12, pl **13**
Nardoo, 60, pl **60**
Native
  Hollyhock, 6
  Myrtle, 42, pl **40**
Nicotinia
  excelsior, 19
  occidentalis, 19, pl **19**
Olearia
  pimeleoides, 10

subspicata, 10, pl **11**
Orobanche cernua var. *australiana*, 40, pl **40**
Owenia
  acidula, 46, pl **47**
  reticulata, 46
Parakeela
  Broad leaved, 15, pl **15**
  Round leaved, 15, pl **15**
Parasitic plants
  Mistletoe, 39, pl **40**
  Quondong, 39, pl **40**
Petalostylis cassioides, 22, pl **22**
Pittosporum phyllireaoides, 46, pl **47**
Pituri, 20, pl **20**
Plectrachne schinzii, 63, pl **63**
Plectanthus intrateranneus, 48, pl **49**
Podolepis jaceoides, 8, pl **9**
Portulaca fibrosa, 15
Psoralea
  australasica, 24
  cinerea, 24, pl **25**
Pterocaulon sphacelatum, 12, pl **14**
Prostanthera striatiflora, 49, pl **49**
Ptilotus
  exaltatus, 15, pl **16**
  helipteroides, 15, pl **16**
  macrocephalus, 15, pl **16**
  obovatus, 17, pl **16**
  polystachys, 17, pl **16**
Radyera ferragei, 6
Rattlepods, 27
Rhagodia nutans, 55, pl **55**
Rostellaria pogonanthera, 48, pl **49**
Rosy Dock, 63
Rulingia magniflora, 54, pl **54**
Rumex vescarius, 63
Rutidosus helichrysoides, 12, pl **14**
Samphire, 56, pl **57**
Santalum
  acuminatum, 40, pl **14**
  lanceolatum, 40, pl **14**
Scaevola
  depauperata, 52
  ovalifolia, 52, pl **52**
Scleroleana limbata, 56, pl **57**
Seed
  Nine Awn, pl **61**
  Speargrass, 61
  Three awn, 61
Senecio
  gregorii, 8
  lautus, 8, pl **9**
  magnificus, 8, pl **9**

Solanum
  ellipticum, 18, pl **19**
  quadricaulatum, 18, pl **19**
  tuberosum, 18
South Apple, 46, pl **47**
Spinifex
  Feathertop, 60, pl **63**
  Gummy, 63, pl **63**
  Lobed, 63, pl **63**
  Silvery, 63, pl **63**
Stemodia
  glabra, 50, pl **50**
  floribunda, 50
  viscosa, 50
Sturts Desert Rose, 6
Swainsona
  canescens, 24
  microphylla, 24, pl **25**
  phacoides, 24
  procumbens, 24, pl **25**
  swainsonioides, 24, pl **25**
Teucrium racemosum, 49, pl **49**
Themeda australis, 61, pl **60**
Thryptomene maisonneuvi, 34, pl **34**
Tribulus occidentalis, 58, pl **59**
Trichodesma zeylanicum, 20, pl **20**
Triodia
  basedowii, 62, pl **63**
  irritans, 63, pl **63**
  pungens, 63, pl **63**
Wahlenbergia
  communis, 51, pl **51**
  gracilis, 51
Wattle
  Elegant, 31
  Round Leaf, 31, pl **30**
  Maitlands, 31, pl **31**
  Western Myall, 29, pl **28**
Wild
  Gooseberry, 18, pl **19**
  Orange, 38, pl **38**
  Tobacco, 19
  Tomato, 18, pl **19**
  Stock, 18, pl **19**
Vittidinia, 11
Zygochloa paradoxa, 62, pl **62**
Zygophyllum howittii, 58, pl **59**

NB Helipterum now Rodanthe
Helichrysum now Bracteantha, Crysocephalum, Leucocephalum & Schoenia
Craspedia now Pycnosorus
Cassia now Senna
Clianthus now Swainsona